Wordclay 1663 Liberty Drive, Suite 200
Bloomington, IN 47403 www.wordclay.com
© Copyright 2008 Jennifer Whitaker. All rights reserved.
No part of this book may be reproduced, stored in a retrieval system, or transmitted by any means without the written permission of the author.
First published by Wordclay on 3/21/2008.
Printed in the United States of America.
This book is printed on acid-free paper.

Emotional Rollercoaster: Young Adulthood
By Jennifer A. Whitaker

MY LOVE

Unto my love I announce
That he is the greatest gift
For me, a girl said.
Standing in a white gown she was,
As she waited for him to come out of his hiding place.
In the black darkness he stood
As he waited for her,
For he was a shy man,
Low self-esteem he behold.
While the girl walked forward to the preacher's office
she found the love of her life.
The most well loved and
Most loving man she dreamed,
With a muscular build.
Older than she, he was,
But at same maturity he was too.
For these reasons he received lots of love from her.
"May we be together forever?" I ask you now
For I am the women in the story you just read.
You my love, are as majestic as they come.
May we walk down the aisle of majesty together today?
I love you.

Time to Vanish or Live

Out of the darkness came a broken women
from her lonesome house.
She ran as she tried to catch her dreams.
With her dreams, would the love of her life
vanish, too?
Down on her knees she fell
longing to regain the love she once enjoyed.
From lover to lover she jumped
looking for the one to spend a lifetime with.
It was until a day in June of 2007.
On this very day she met a lover
she longed to meet.
Longing for a life together
they still do.
As she works hard to pursue a degree
to support a family, she asks,
"will I ever be able to make one
with my love?"
If the lover is never found
so death may come her way
in a lonely time
leaving her by satin's side.

Christmas 2007

From Distance apart Came two hearts.
At one time they were one,
Later separated By a stubborn mind
Leaving one heart broken
and Another heart dyeing.
A stubborn mind That refused to straighten up
Began to not only take the life of one,
But of three hearts.
Bad choices came from the mind
Only to lead to a torn life walking down the path to death.
The only reason the heart still lived
Was the love that came from another unrecognized.
Continuing to feed the mind she did,
But the two broken hearts still remained miles away.
It was over a year later before the mind had healed.
It healed just enough to realize that she had affected them.
When the mind came back to reunite with reality,
she realized how much she was loved. I
n the treatment she began to realize
all these feelings that the two broken hearts were only trying to control her,
Were misleading by the idea of "Feelings are

Facts."
As the mind recognized this lesson,
She realized she was manic and totally out of it for a year straight.
"What happen to my life the mind questioned?"
It seemed as though the only way back to the right path
Was to listen to the broken hearts.
Even more to all recognize the endless love they had for her the whole time.
The two hearts offered the mind a chance to come back,
A time where they could all heal together,
And be together as a family again.
It is the three of us again.
Out in the garden the mind goes to get dirty,
To find the broken women waiting to play in the flowers.
In the spring they rush before it's too late.
It was Christmas before the mind came back as the daughter.
It was that holiday when she was able to hang out in the kitchen,
To learn to cook with the women.
Both bonded over the boiling pot of chili.
It was the same winter when the daughter's car needed work.
The broken man stopped toughening it up

breaking into tears on top of his daughters hood.
Sitting during break they bonded again as "Bigdaddy and Laney."
It was meant to be a fun holiday this year to teach us that there is more to Christmas than presents.
The meaning of family was proven this year.
The three hearts come back to be one again.
As the story went on the daughter re-enrolled into college.
As much as health improved,
she was as she was finally able to hold a job.

The Race

Sitting by the fire
my heart begins to speed
On a road to nowhere.
Followed by a hike in blood pressure
they began the race of a lifetime.
The pounding of my heart began feeling like a sudden burst from nowhere.
It gave no warning.
With loads of excitement, she laid down.
Hyperness welcome my way.
Hyperness is my friend,
I say As it releases the stress and anxiety in

the moment.
With my eyes closed,
sitting near the fire,
I began to picture the three teams,
Hearts, Blood and overwhelmness,
racing at the Bristol Speedway.
What else does it take to take the life of a man.?
Once a heart is removed, the blood speeds away.
The life is followed by the removal of the soul.
Death stay away! I demand,
as it is an unwelcome journey.
I am on a journey to nowhere.
I fight out of determination to get somewhere in life.
May my life be returned so I can have a change to get somewhere,
A change to be somebody.
I once was someone I am no longer.
Determined to be the champion,
win the race of a life and death,
Like my Grandmother did surviving her open heart surgery.
You are my hero Grandma.
You won your race and continue to fight to this very day.
May I continue to battle my race winning and

Live to be a hero to my grandkids like you.
Death I cast you away Unto the pits of hell.
You will never take my heart as it is my source of life.
My heart does not belong to you,
But to the God above who created it.

A Letter to Mom

Remembering life alone.
It is such a hard thing to accept.
It was not but a few years ago
that you came into my life.
You and Dad became one.
A Mother you became,
a loner you no longer were.
You held up a wall for years after being hurt so bad,
Dad was the first to break your wall.
What an angel I thought you were,
as you rapped your arm around me that evening.
I had a long hard life at the time,
behind me it went,
as you brought me into your arms
and made me somebody.
A lonely soul I was,
but a loved daughter I became.
You may be my step-mother,

but by heart you mean something more,
with your heart of gold.
As of now ,
I am days away from you halfway ,
across the country,
hoping to see you over the holidays.
What is it that has made you such a good women?
Is it the love of the living God?
So Dad says.
If it is true,
you have been a great example ,
teaching me to be a real lady.
I grew up as a tomboy,
yet with you,
I learn more about being women.
You are the difference in my life,
so may you reach out this way and be my mommy once again.
"I Love you", I say with all thanksgiving to Grandma for bringing you into this world.

Why Am I so Grateful for My Parents?

"Why am I so grateful for you?" you ask,
Because you made a difference in my life.
As a unstable kid with problems every left and right,
All I had going good, was the love of a father,

that later,
brought in to my life the love of a mother.
I had a childhood, filled with hardships.
There were many times I was made fun of,
times I was hurt physically and emotionally,
I had friends that would come and go,
but there was one that was always there.
This was you Daddy.
As many burdens I put on you,
as much stress I pushed your way,
you would never hurt me
or even think about rejecting me the way my other family did.
I was lost for years not knowing who I was,
what to do in life,
where to go,
but it was you that cleared my path
and healed my broken heart.
You, Dad,
are the main source of love in my life.
You are only tied with the love of my second mom
whom you were sure would love me before you brought her into my torn life.
She too,
helped clear the way for me to have a better life.
Both of you have allowed me to go to my dream

school,
to go for my dream field ,
and to more importantly,
become who I want to become with the help of
your love and support.
You are very special people that will one day
need my help.
If I may be there by your side then and there
that day.
If there was a parent appreciation day ,
I would celebrate it with you
with joy each and every year,
only to try to let you know
how much you are appreciated,
and what a difference you have made in my
life.
I love you.

Kissy Sleeps

As I manage to open my eyes,
I begin to see your face.
Looking my way, as you always are,
I sit up to see you twisted.
Like a mini tornado, you sleep in a circle.
Breathing soft tender gasps of air,
You calm me.
In my warm waterbed,

we both snuggle as I set it high heat.
In my bed we both lie as the summer goes by.
In the depth of the night we sleep.
When I am filled with anxiety all I do is call your name
followed behind by the attendance of you to my care.
When I am alone you come to see me.
When I leave, you are certain to say bye.
In my room we always gather
to snuggle everyday I am home.
As the days go by,
we live to see the night when we can return
to bed to see each other.
Your sweet face I watch go to sleep
before I lay back myself.
A kiss on the head you get every night
before I lay back to go to sleep
to the beautiful sound of your sweet gasps
of air each and every night.
This is the beauty of night between me and you.
You are as majestic of a princess I could ever find.
May your heart shines through each
and every day. You were
My love day one,
when I first saw you sleeping

at the head of the bed with your momma.
It was on the day we met
in the summer of 2001.
Hear my letter,
and know just how much you are loved and appreciated.
I love you with all my heart.

What's Love?

Lying in bed, I long to see you,
as I toss and turn in times of loneliness.
I wait to hear your manly voice call my name,
your warm arms to reach out for me,
and longing for a day in time
when I will be lonely no more.
As of today,
I am alone in a room of my own.
The only thing I have coming my way speaks
another language,
with the only similarity being
it, too, is a mammal.
It, my sweet,
can not satisfy all my needs like you.
I miss your compassion,
the heart you have for me,
your willingness to work,
to care for me,

and allow me to live my dreams.
The heart you have has told me something special,
not to worry about the money,
but to follow my dreams.
If I never make another dime,
you would love me just as much.
What more is there to you than a truly loving Christian man?
Are you the man of my dreams?
That I ask as I have many dreams, emotions,
and thoughts of you flying across my mind.
Listening to music,
of a women who wasted her life in the bar,
drinking alcohol, messing with her mind,
I wonder, Are you so majestic of a man that you can provide me with the structured life I need?
That I need because with you,
my life will not be wasted in this hospital,
but rather spent at home loving you,
As we develop memories together.
I have a pathway in front of me
that slowly unwinds
as I spend time with you.
Only the love of a man can unlock the door of my cage
Releasing me into his arms

to take home and care.
The question is, are you that man?

Thank you for reading my book. I hope you enjoyed it. If you did, purchase Emotional Rollercoaster: Young Adulthood Part 1 and continue the venture you started. I will be releasing Part 1 January of 2019, if not before. Stay in touch with me on my blog at

https://acemycourse.net/blog-streampage/

Share with me your experience, opinion, feedback, and any ideas of future books I write. Subscribe to my blog to stay in tune and be one of the first to receive the announcement when Part 1 is finally released. I am working on Part 2 now so do not wait. There is tons more excitement coming your way. Be on the watch!

Incase you wonder, I am an educator with 18 years in the field. I have my Bachelors in Accounting and Graduate Studies in Accounting. That said, as I am owner of a tutoring company, I always welcome new ideas, including any type of knowledge you would like me to write a book covering. I am a Business Consultant, Accountant, Author, and Tutor all in one. I will

Flip the page ready to imagine, understand and feel the life of a teenager from inside the their mind. As we all go through dramatic high and low points in life, especially as teenagers and/or young adults, we have all see what you will read. Though we each see the same event in many ways, the way I describe, will help parents, grandparents, and older siblings, understand modern day young adults. Overtime, life and culture has changed. What is normal now, was not 10 years ago. With technology came a new culture. As you read, consider how you can apply it to your life. This is rather you are the young adult, or the family trying to understand. It will be an asset in some form or another to the family as a whole.

It is based on what I had to live through as a child, preteen and young adult. As I am still in my early twenties, I am still living the results of a lot of what happen in my early days, though there is also a lot that has been resolved. Through these ups and downs I have created numerous poems to reach out to the world of unheard voices and let them know I am hear to speak for you and let you know you are not alone.

write a book based on any related topic or subcategory that you request. Though my expertise are in Business and/or Accounting, I have a passion to spread my knowledge, even if it means my secrets to success. I am including you when I say it.

Thank you once again for reading my Sample of Emotional Rollercoaster: Young Adulthood. I look forward to hearing from you.

inquiry@acemycourse.net

*Email me a request for a copy any time to be added to the "First to Get a Copy" list. Discounts, bonus money and more available to all on the waiting list between now and day of release.

It is Summer of 2018, we are at the countdown of Part 1 Release! Be Ready!

CPSIA information can be obtained
at www.ICGtesting.com
Printed in the USA
LVRC020920180619
621460LV00011BA/63